My First Picture Joke Book

Shoo Rayner

PUFFIN BOOKS

Why do birds fly south in the winter?

Because it's too far to walk.

Why does a lion wear a furry coat?

Because he'd look stupid in a red plastic raincoat.

What's worse than a giraffe with a sore throat?

A centipede with blisters.

How do you know if carrots are good for your eyesight?

Have you ever seen a rabbit wearing glasses?

What animals need oiling?

Mice, because they squeak.

Why do tigers eat raw meat?

Because they don't know how to cook.

How does a dentist examine a crocodile's teeth?

Very carefully!

What's big and ugly and has red spots all over it?

A monster with measles.

What do you do if there's a gorilla in your bed?

Sleep somewhere else.

How do you catch a monkey?

Hang upside down in a tree and pretend you're a banana.

What do you call a monkey with two bananas in his ears?

You can call him anything because he can't hear you.

What do you get if you cross a cow with an octopus?

Something that can milk itself.

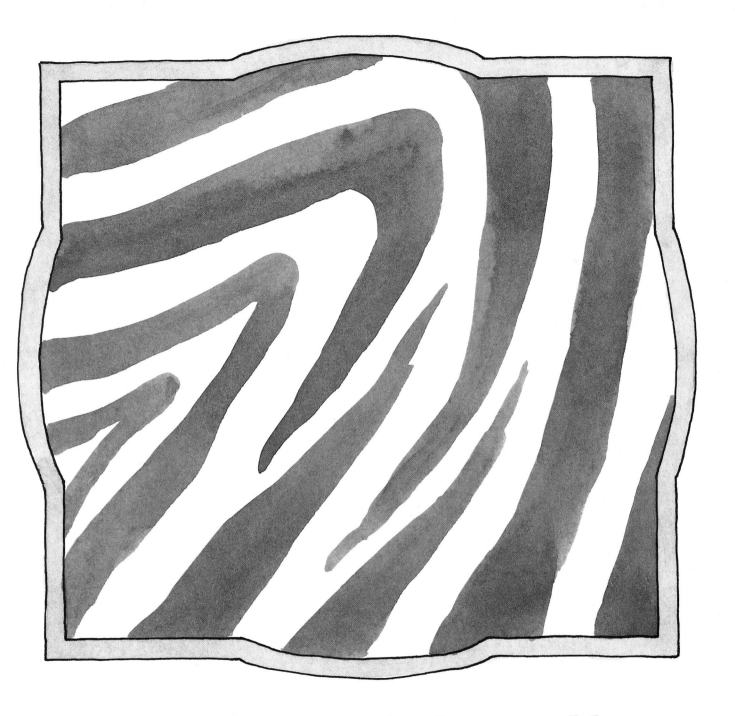

What is black and white and has sixteen wheels?

A zebra on roller skates.

How does an elephant get up an oak tree?

He stands on an acorn and waits for it to grow.

What do you get if you cross an elephant with a kangaroo?

Great big holes all over Africa.